WHAT BOOKS PRESS

AN IMPRINT OF

THE GLASS TABLE

COLLECTIVE

LOS ANGELES

ALSO BY JAN WESLEY

Only So Much
Living in Freefall
A Closeness of Vision
Running Out of Altitude

IT WASN'T ALWAYS LIKE THIS

IT WASN'T ALWAYS LIKE THIS

POEMS

JAN WESLEY

WHAT
BOOKS
PRESS

LOS ANGELES

Library of Congress Cataloging-in-Publication Data

Names: Wesley, Jan author
Title: It wasn't always like this : poems / Jan Wesley.
Other titles: It was not always like this
Description: Los Angeles : What Books Press, 2025. | Summary: "This
    collection of poems is marked by intimate reckonings and unexpected
    departures. The wisdoms and raw resilience of the speaker combine to
    exhilarate the reader"-- Provided by publisher.
Identifiers: LCCN 2025036254 | ISBN 9798998905551 paperback
Subjects: LCGFT: Poetry
Classification: LCC PS3623.E779 I8 2025
LC record available at https://lccn.loc.gov/2025036254

Cover art: Gronk, *Untitled*, mixed media on paper, 2023
Book design by Ash Good, www.ashgood.com
Author photo: Wayne Shimabukuro

What Books Press
363 South Topanga Canyon Boulevard
Topanga, CA 90290

WHATBOOKSPRESS.COM

CONTENTS

III

FOREWORD
THE VENICE COLLECTIVE ON JAN WESLEY'S POEMS

As with all her books, *It Wasn't Always Like This* bristles with energy. A poet of consummate skill, Jan Wesley invites the reader into immersive explorations that are deeply personal yet wholly human. Among the highlights is the splendidly unexpected and daring use of narrative in "My Beautiful Car." Throughout, her writing overflows with language rich and unique; its long sentences weave and roll like a grouping of waves in the open sea, undaunted by the coming shore.

Jan was a much-loved member of our collective—cheerful, smart, compassionate, generous, dedicated, willing to take risks. And who didn't welcome the Muffin Tops she brought to our workshops? She did everything abundantly, whether sky diving, fast cars, or poetry. More than anyone I know, she lived life to the fullest. I miss her daily, and carry her in my mind and heart.

—*Jeanette Clough*

———————

Jan was one of my first poetry friends in Los Angeles; we spent years touring (and EATING at) the city's vast array of restaurants; she met my remarkable father as I met hers; we shared a vast array of ideas regarding changing the world. Like many, I prompted her to be a teacher. We spent—it felt like— forever talking about poetry, fiction, our families, our lovers, our friends, our hopes and our dreams. Her early passing leaves a huge emptiness.

—*Marjorie Becker*

———————

Electric with verve, Jan Wesley's final collection (how it hurts to write "final") is as dynamic, engaging, original and unforgettable as Jan herself. Here's a poet "playing with both hands," as poet/critic Bill Mohr might say—with thrilling command, wedded to a nervy taste for risk, craft equal to the sheer force of experience that these poems so willingly share. The life splayed across these pages is a worthy mirror of the real life of our beloved friend. Losing her remains a shock.

Jan's courage, encouragement, generosity, smarts, friendship and support have been critical to me, especially as I returned to poetry—and I feel lucky to have shared a path that included the mentorship of David St. John in Venice & LA, Ralph Angel and David Wojahn via Vermont College, our dear longtime workshop-mates, and many warm adventures, both personal and poetic. She was a trailblazer. We're lucky, at least, to have this one last gift in our hands. With love . . .

—*Sarah Maclay*

The last conversation I had with Jan was when we were standing on the sidewalk near Holaday's place and she was telling me about her car, parked across the street. She said the last ticket she got was when she was going … some triple digit. She looked at her car with such pride that it could go that fast. She said the officer was surprised when he saw her as the driver. We smiled and nodded at that shared experience and then stared at her car in awe and silence for a few minutes.

She talked about the order of dying, of leaving people behind, and, she said, "This isn't what I expected would happen." Then she laughed her Jan laugh, shrugged, and said something like, "Well, y'never know, do you."

—*Dina Hardy*

We are having dinner, Jan Wesley and I, on the rooftop of a hotel in downtown Barcelona. It's September 2023. She nibbles. The city lights glisten. There is a loud party across the street. *You have told me about this,* she says, *people having dinner so late here. I want to travel more. Perhaps coming back to*

Barcelona, or going a to a smaller town in the South, and learn Spanish. Seville, Granada. Or going to France. Someone said that you can take the train from Barcelona to Paris, it's just six hours, I think; and you don't have to deal with the hassle of airports. Or I could rent a car and drive to Paris, you know how much I like cars and driving. I should get a studio, a small studio, I don't need much, and write. I have so many unfinished poems, if we can call them poems, and of course writing new ones, too. Should we order some coffee or herbal tea? Not sure if this is exactly what she says. Memory is an act of imagination. But I still can hear her voice, like the voice in her poems: the rhythm, the speed, the strength, the complexity, that desire of moving forward. And I still can see her talking, making plans, unafraid, perched on a roof top on the Mediterranean.

—*Mariano Zaro*

I had the privilege to be in the workshop at Midnight Special from the first day Jan showed up. Over the years I've witnessed her dazzling poetry and her detailed and passionate critiques. Her generosity and talent as a poet were integral to the workshop and the salon, not to mention our lives. All I can say is, "Thank you, Jan."

—*Paul Lieber*

Jan was a dynamo, a tornado…and a total sweetheart. You couldn't help but love her passion and fearlessness. I didn't really know Jan the film editor or the skydiver—only Jan as poet, friend, and literary co-conspirator. She was the welcoming face I remember most from my first Saturday afternoon at the Midnight Special workshop back in the late 1990s. Over all those years since, through myriad readings and events, and poring over countless, ever more personal poems together in workshop sessions, Jan was there emanating her special jagged energy, laughing that crow laugh.

Once, when I lived in Arizona, Jan called me from Interstate 10. She was driving back to LA after attempting to live in Austin and was wondering about where to get gas. We talked all the way across that empty stretch west of Phoenix until she got to the truck stop a few miles before the California border. She could have landed that plane herself—or jumped—but I was glad I could be there in the control tower to get her safely down.

—*Jim Natal*

Jannie was one of my first workshop pals. Her smile welcomed then as it did the last time I saw her. She remained radically open, inclusive, warm, and wise even as she faced death head on. Her loss has created a void—in me, in us, in poetry and in radicals everywhere.

—*Brenda Yates*

I don't know how long ago, but many years back, as Jan Wesley, Mariano Zaro, and I walked through the *L.A. Times* Festival of Books, Jan shared a struggle she was having. Maybe she wanted to give up poetry, or maybe write prose, or maybe just go traveling. What happened? Instead of giving up, Jan kept going. She parlayed her unique style into the gorgeous, skilled, vulnerable, dense, and ferocious prose poems we get to cherish in this, her final collection.

She always showed up, took risks, went for the truth, the bone and marrow, the heart, body, mind, every fiber, muscle—noun, verb, adjective. She lived and shared from the generous non-conformist wellspring of deep capacity won only from surviving pain and refusing to become closed and cranky. I take a lesson from her. I carry her inside me and say, "Oh, get over yourself, Holaday. Just do your best and keep going." She did, and it helped me. She still helps me. I loved and love her. Thank you Jannie, bright star.

—*Holaday Mason*

"Try to remember it always," he said once Gogol had reached him. *"Remember that you and I made this journey, that we went together to a place where there was nowhere left to go."*

The Namesake
Jhumpa Lahiri

|

WHAT WE MEAN ABOUT THE LOVE OF A LIFE

I am allergic to coconut and cat hair. When we broke up, he sent me a tuft of orange cat fur and a coconut box label taped to a piece of cardboard jammed into an envelope. It was brilliant. It was art. The last time I saw him years had gone by and I walked up behind him where he perused a shelf of CDs, his spine lengthened by taut muscles inside a cotton-blend sky-blue shirt and I still knew the sway of his torso, a slight rise in the left shoulder, and I don't remember, but I probably gave a good sigh to his ass, corduroy pants tight around his legs that always had a savvy instinct to run. When he broke up with me, or the me unable to give up the pending lifestyle I didn't imagine I would regret, there was the sense that love would never be the same. The day we met, he leaned back in his chair on its two rear legs and looked at me walking up to him not giving a shit whether I was stylish or distracted or young, or whether he was interested, available, or kind. We had been set up for what most people would imagine was a date but for us it was all about changing the system. His eyes studied the world and its roaming clans through window-thick glasses with one stem taped to the frame. We lived on a hill choked off by a five-lane boulevard lined with ethnic restaurants and shops that stayed open late because people had nowhere else to go. We were poor but not like people who didn't stand a chance. He and I could read contracts and choose not to make raw deals that would take things out from under us. We could con our way into jobs and always make a few bucks for gas and food. Our bodies were shoots pushing up from the dirt. We were lion-hearted, laden with limberness. We were just beginning.

THE BREAKERS

I heave a load of dry wood in a leather sling
into the garage, restack shoulder-wide logs
for fires we will never set as another winter fades.

And you *were* the one
until you weren't.

The wood is stacked.
One piece shifts and the pile collapses

to the concrete floor, sounds of percussion
tiny squeaks and pops like a break of failing reeds.

I dig for keys and drive to the jetty along
wave after wave until you aren't the one

until a release of our venom. The rocks are slick with
constant misty spray from turmoil

of water breaking at will,
sending stinky air. Creatures

in shiny creamy hair that isn't really hair
slither and speak in mariner talk. I drape over
a boulder not knowing which rock

was *our* rock. But that was then and now I slip on
bird grease, the gulls and seals dragging me

farther out from the breakers until I fall away.

IN MY SOLITUDE

Sun rays have just begun to fall
across a corner of the terrace where I sit
with coffee and her new book I envy, and hate
to feel that way, vengeful like unyielding
scratch of nails down an arm so I kick
myself for it, but it's a good book
and deserves the glory it gets. I lean
against the railing seven floors above a park
along a side street where looking down
inspires restraint and I back off
from tipping into space toward the ground,
its certainty unforgiving. It seems
to be sunset, the heat of August winding down
in this holy time of the fight to do what
the body wants instead of what the body
gives into. There is a field of green
grass in the park that stays open to people
without homes and nurturing trees have shade,
bodies slow across the grass searching
to resettle themselves under different trees
as the light moves around the sky. Men
and women we avoid, the people we never
get to know, sit on their jackets and their minds
are whittled, flimsy plastic bags stuffed
with all they own. From inside the house I hear
a jazz singer float a song and I breathe in
my solitude, the book tapping on my thigh
as she speaks only to me and I sit with her
ablaze in her stories so hot to the touch.

ALL FALL DOWN

The stems of plants droop
from their waists, their sweet juices

going bad but not quite to ruin. Cop sirens
drown the racket of confusion and doubt

and who is the man with silver
shoes who steps out of a blue car. A chill

embarrasses the skin in a land of heat. Life
is vicarious adventures now: birds

smothering trees; the errors of my actions
drowning out a god who can't change

my situation. I sink into predictable nightfall,
the house opaque as I move with staccato

touch along the wall across a pile of unread
books, every step dragged by animal instinct.

A man I was told loved me repeated daily
mantras, imperfect with his loose love hung

by a thread into winter, into separate corners,
a punch of obedience on black ice—

betrayal of balance cranked around every corner.

A SHORT STORY ABOUT LOVE

At a lucky parking spot in the lot my ex
hangs his head, bowed over his phone. As I scrutinize
him I choke at imperceptible ways he might raise

his face to check his car waiting for him like a pet,
loyal & soothing. He is no longer someone I want
to take time to be polite to, to make digestible chat with.

It is windy and I cannot trust myself to keep anger at bay,
not the day to be usual and pile explosive emotions
into his trunk, overflowing, junked up, locked and private.

He lingers and I am fastened to a life we
managed to be right with sometimes, kisses behind
my knees. I bend into my own car door with a click

to secure the belt as I check his progress. His one foot is
cocked behind his calf, his back agile as he leans
lusciously into his own body. With my mind groggy

and halting, I check him out, turn the key, throw it
into reverse & back out the way a cat flees, the man I loved
dangerously close to lifting his eyes as the end

of us flashes in my mirror, his finger on *delete*, light nudging
his temple like a gun, *that* guy my mother warned me of—
stealthy, criminal, flying in from the wrong side of town.

DANCING IN THE LIVING ROOM

When my mother told me to take it off,
I knew it was my kind of music.
                                        —Jeff Beck

I was limber like animals in trees,
danced up to my mother like James Brown, dangling
her car keys, pleading my rock-solid case that there was nothing more dire
than grabbing the wheel to drive me to buy my first LP.
And she did, and we parked in front of a monstrous box-store that changed
the way cities shopped the way appliances changed the frequency
            of home-cooked meals.
She slipped me five bucks and waited by the curb, perhaps
remembering songs she knew, like *Funny Valentine*,
the times her fleet feet slid around a room with men
who loved her before I was born.

THE TRUTH ABOUT DANGER

Birds know the science of flying. The wind is important. What exhales from blue sky's breath skates underneath their wings, no motor, no blades, beautiful music when they call to one another, no grammar, all tone shifts, mother birds gathering seeds, the dull sides of the sticks. Tonight a crow flares and drops below the hood of my car, and my gasp is raspy, wordless. No thump, no bird cry, no whimpering, Just gone. I pull over to the shoulder and see the wing as it stays still, feathers fluttering their last. An aging athlete who knows what pain is, said *everyone has aches and pain. If you don't, you didn't play.*

IMPORTANCE OF PLACE AND LEAVING IT AT THAT

There are things I never say, and then some
days a desire to spill the messy glut of dramas
you left me with boils over. It went beyond giving up
the house on Sherman Canal with Judy Collins'
face on the wall up against the deck, painted by a man
captivated as he put her in that place, her blue eyes
like a blue underneath ice and hair swept away
from her face and quiet and lips that let go of the music
like a slow draw of silk from her mouth. Life mocks
us claiming *it could be worse,* or *you did the best*
you knew, tedious clichés like fingers sunk in cement
and the days you grabbed my hair, the slap from ear
to ear that burned during days you rocked me
out of our small boat into the shallow water of the canal
where you wanted me to believe we lived
in Venice, Italy rather than the blip of land a mile
from the Pacific Ocean. I should have known our world
was wrong when we raised havoc instead of kids,
and me a fool as I wallowed in shame and surrendered to
joy. When I called you one night wondering
if you'd be home in time for dinner and maybe
a movie, a woman picked up the phone and asked me
who I was and I said, *wife,* as though that could mean
what I thought it could mean. I began to prowl around
our home, the one after they took down
the Judy Collins' place, to know that you were gone
as if I could rearrange the unusable space you left inside.
It was spring and nasty moss had grown along
the patio where I discovered relief in having

left it at that, where you would come toward me
with some kind of odd embrace to remake me, to paint me
into a corner of the railing and sigh, *you, you are so
beautiful*, and I'd say, *you, you don't know love at all.*

LIGHTS OUT

I change my mind the way a manual transmission changes gears. My car is like this, stick shift that makes valets grin when my high-heeled shoes exit the driver's door, the man in his vest with small bowtie swoops to the door, my legs wobbly from an hour in traffic, and he extends his hand to mine as if we are aristocracy. Nathan taught me generosity, I taught him resistance to the worst in us, sometimes silence, the art of peace. It was another century when my mother pulled me onto the curb as a taxi sped toward my foot ready to run to the other side of the street, her eyes more terrified than I knew how to be. Sometimes it's simple. Joy is. Last night I heard music everywhere I went. In the grocery store they're piping out a playlist of old tunes in front of the cheese case. I take a good walk home, pumping my sack of food with a weight that grows my biceps. I think about age, illness, injury, perhaps anger that digs a thumb into temples on the sides of my head. In the time of *then*, I would yank a sweater over my head, quick strides to the car to somewhere, but that is hazy memory now. I sit on the edge of the bed, final light of the sun through the blinds, skin dry, bones complaining. A dictionary thick book of short stories spreads open, tells me these are one hundred, the best of all time. Some are wise, some exaggerate who is smart, who did something unforgivable.

OFFSPRING OF A SUICIDE

She was impatient to leave, and I was nineteen, people eager to say that her disinterest to slide a foot into a slipper or take the mail to the curb was better *than the alternative*. I knew she was going to take her life, perhaps miss a stop sign or fall asleep at the stove. There is tremendous loss in the hills today, thousands of acres of trees and moss and ivy and deer and creatures smaller than cats, so many people's shelters sheared from history by murderous fire. There is loss sometimes of music, of geese migrating over the reservoir, but there is also kindness, like her fingers that combed through my hair, pitchers of peonies or dogwood branches she arranged on my desk as though she was the maker of all things. *Wonder*, she would say, *wonder what things do, who the animals trust, what people mean when they love you.* She would pat my back like a drummer to urge me on to forge passion into its rightful place before the lack of it could do me in. The day the phone rang I knew she was dead. I sat on the steps of the admin building to watch people trail as if the glide of their movement might ease my grief until I had to return to the Golden State of opportunity and celebrity, one foot dragging the other onto an airplane, taking off into weather and miles of fresh snow slathering the mountains.

DAY IN A SOMETIMES LIFE

Woke up, fell out of bed
Dragged a comb across my head
Found my way downstairs and drank a cup
And looking up I noticed I was late.
　　　　　—Lennon and McCartney, "A Day in the Life"

PCH, nine a.m. Big Rock turn-off where he leaves my package on right front tire of a Bentley halfway up the drive and three quick spikes of fine white powder drawn along the sheen of the mirror jolts my nose and shocks me like one-night stands who change personality after sex all night. This is how it snows without weather: tiny clicks of ragged nails keeping time to ballads; a color palette streaked across the sky; shimmer and sheen on the ocean. Then my car creeps toward security guards who nod me through the floral gate into the Twentieth Century Studio. 9:45 a.m. week five with four days off, hours in a whir through the cinema of violence as it screams. I give away tickets to once-in-a-lifetime concert, call my date and say *date is off, call me soon*, blow a kiss through the phone. We screen another scene of a bullet through the actor's brain to show, to know with certainty, the man is dead. Dead-tired, I follow myself with the relief of release that lets me go home. I kick my shoes off in the parking lot, walk in bare feet to my car, the last person gone, air like glass. The night is opaque, and house lights flick on, mouth so dry I drink underneath the faucet, count the seconds as the nightly train wails through 21st and Hoover, sound of the rails fading where I walk across the kitchen, graze the edge of a dining room chair. Mail gets tossed, food-to-go left for tomorrow, sliding door to balcony thrown back for wine above the city, my weariness like toes through sand, and I miss him again, reach under my shirt, unhook my bra, all clothes flung, fall into bed. My head hovers above sleep in mystical suspension before I collapse, plummet, and surrender.

NEW YORK TO LOS ANGELES NONSTOP 2002

The gift he slipped me at the mouth of the subway before a farewell dinner on Bleeker Street sits like a soothing stone in my fur-lined pocket, our table with picked-over food facing a depleted skyline, his building twelve blocks north of where the towers fell. A cabbie takes me to Newark, snow cloaking the runways as every plane gets wings de-iced by men craned around in foul-weather gear. By 12 a.m. my spine gives in to seat 21A that crushes like a glove. I sleep and wake in the flight path humming over patch-work farmland, sculpted canyons, mountain ranges almost scratching the belly of the plane. Hypnotic voices wake me, a chaos of lights growing closer and closer, swimming pools lolling in luxury with heated blue bottoms steaming in the night. A thump of the hull welcomes me to Los Angeles, the pilot's voice sultry with fatigue as he speaks the final instructions, and I am home. The man in New York City does not go home, has one more drink as I wait to alight on this outsized microchip steaming in chemicals. Faces and necks move around the brain stem to fetch items stowed and shifted in flight, the man's lips unloosing my name, and the jet is slow into the gate with nose low to the ground sniffing the urban oasis like a dog.

ATMOSPHERIC RIVERS

The sound of electricity hums after the rains in this deviant winter drilled by jackhammers of wind and chill that fire tiny needles at the eyes. Avalanches of water change into snow on distant peaks to meet a glistening horizon and a blimp—airship of quiet cruise—as it glides over celebrations of the new year. Forecasters bemoan the unrestrained cold, our bodies tossed under comforters, feet in socks on hardwood floors, landslides invading our homes.

I make a breakfast with a basket of pastries on the side to soothe fear and dread, the walls of windows peeking onto a hawk enviable in its flight, a week of downpour filling up empty riverbeds. Brooding overcast surrounds me where I step out to weave through odors of the aftermath of rain, a relief that feels like the touch of a lover's skin, and again I care for others better than I do for myself, a sacrifice that might get me into a heaven I don't believe in.

Believing in the sky, my hands are nervous in my pockets and I stop short where a coyote stares at me gazing back at him. I speak as if we are friends, and say, *the hills have water now, you will find food,* as he comes close enough to lick my hand until we remember who we are. I assure him, *we can protect life. I will plant vegetables and peonies for the spring,* but really what I'll do is rise over the earth to imagine what lies hidden under the skin of a field that isn't meant to be a field.

ENVY

There is cleaving along the coastline,
a couple walking past the waves with lifetimes
of evolution scrolling between them. Their eyes
track the dented cove where dogs mangle
snakes of seaweed. Quivering snouts

drag a slab of driftwood beneath cliffs,
its soil withering in erosion at alarming rates.
The woman's neck loosens and her
hair falls onto the man's shoulder
the couple nuzzled for warmth. I watch

their mouths speak without bicker, words
uttered from one mouth that recognizes one other.

A dozen surfers hike out of the ocean
in seal suits. The couple walks to the wood stairs
to the road where stretches of cars wait
along the deadly Coast Highway. She chatters

close to his ear, and I hear my lover's ambush
this morning—a desire to change our course
that no longer re-centers itself. We have

surrendered to the damage between us,
those echoes that *people who love do not
become silent,* and yes, it's true, I have. I follow
the couple along the shoreline, stones broken underfoot

fumbling for my keys where so many SUVs are
bloated like they've taken in salt. The couple brushes
sand from one another's flesh, lovesick and fogged
in a steam of the feverish breath they disappear into.

AFTER RAYMOND CARVER
AT MIDNIGHT

The darkness felt like a hood and the moon fell behind a cloud, so I turned on the light. We had been drinking scotch on the patio until loping to bed to be able to get up for work and he drifted off to sleep so I hung up my clothes and spotted my flesh with face cream from a company in Germany swearing I'll look a hundred years younger for another hundred years. He dreamed he would leave the two of us and head out like a camel across a desert, knees flexible, leisurely in their gait, knowing how to save water, understanding distance. I carried on reading a story about couples who drank colossal pours of liquor, making me abandon the book, as if the hush of pages might wake him. The silkiness of the sheets sends my leg to touch his leg out of habit, remembrance of the final things he'd said. To have the last word, he makes a final point by saying, *it's like that*, emphasis on *that*. I was bagged under the eyes when he walked to me half-naked in runners' shorts, bent to kiss my head, hand grazing the top of my back. There is an outline of his hand on my spine. *Like that. Baby, it's like that,* my weariness too deep to ask him, *what's like what?* To tell him for the 96th time to stop calling me *baby*.

CRAWLING OUT ON A LIMB

If I wake in the middle of the night, opaque
and bleak, my knee and feet kick off the covers

      into a resurgence of arabesques

into willfulness of flight.
I soar over moon-shine water in another lesser

fall from grace. Today the body
breathes unimpeded air as I rip off my mask.

Beneath, survival is grander than the eye can glean
even as I sink my claws into the bully

        of meaning that treats all pain
like a meal thrown from the window of a car.

Driving beyond another dying storm a breeze

      touches me through the window

where spider design in the glass splits the light
that lifts me by the collar at the furrow of my neck

to let me kiss the sky or kiss this guy who asks

only that we share sweet bread—and just like that
tire tracks down my back disappear like lovely.

JUST TO LET YOU KNOW

…when I first read you, I couldn't get
my mouth around your quagmire of words…

        but I clawed my way through your books
and weather turned crazy in ways
that bring up gush of soil, earthworms,
explosion of cicadas after dark.

        They told me you were fickle
and a little ferocious around the eyes, your spit
of meaning surrounded by a stomp in a loud gait

until we have to duck and weave from what
might feel like a hook across the jaw. Now, no
one's talking smack about you anymore, some of us

stuck in a state of homage, as if you dance on fire,
        like moths around the lamp—
        and truly, madly, I would scramble

to lick the flames and bear the burn even
careful as I am about love and getting taken by guys
I don't deal with anymore. I used to think if you

met a bad end I'd be graveside, sunlight sucked
through the trees and people wondering why
I'd shown up to see you bundled into your last

        darkness and when we might have marked
some covert time like a couple of prisoners smoking,
knowing how to parse each other. Why we

stepped into the dark to sip the milk of headlights
in blades of off-road grass for hours
wrapped in a blanket under stars popping light

like fireflies and you in the quiet whispering I was
your *Lady of Wet Glass-Rings on the Album Cover.*

> *Denis Johnson*
> *1949–2017*

HOW THINGS HAPPEN WE NEVER SEE

When I was a kid I never had to go with other kids
to church, my father always in a dither and declaring
there is no god. My face was sunk into books

in the laundry room, being helper and pest
while I waited for kids to race home from their pews.
And some days I slept late—and one of those days my mother
was gone. Just like that. I went from worry to knowing

she was dead—always—and to this day—feeling lucky
I didn't find her there in their bed, her face perhaps pale,
pinned to a view of the ceiling or fallen to the side. I never
saw where her hands had settled, where her beautiful legs

were frozen under the sheet. I hadn't grown enough
imagination to see how my father approached her, what startled
sounds came out of his mouth, how he bent to her,
and if he knew right away or if he tried to wake her or if he

held her or took her hand or if the sun slithered through
the back yard window into the room. Perhaps inertia woke him
as he slept beside her on that Sunday I got up late, ignoring
my chores and giving up patience to wait for the boys.

A haze like the blanch of my skin crept through summer, autumn,
the years. On this day of rest, I leave the bed as the living
plants show off red blooms, and the cat lifts his head, arching,
knowing if I sedated my vigilance we could sleep until noon.

INSOMNIA

I try forgetting
what Isaac Singer says
about leaving the self
out of his writing in stormy
reverence for third person
narrative and the hush
of night is tinny
like a chattering yammer
of voices. Dispatched
headlines talk out loud
about the government
— those warriors we'd like
to silence before more
countries lumber to their knees.
I never look at a child
without thoughts of what
the child looks like
injured, obsessive thinking
about wayward friends
and neighbors bending
to fix things and dropping
their guards. Your eyes
are burdened with REM
sleep and I could write
page after page of a story
that refuses to be about us
but you promised me
lunch and it'll be me
who packs the grapes,
tomatoes & bread, a spread

of Camembert, linen cloth
to shake out between us.
I cup my hands over
the shadows of your face
and take in a glint of jacarandas
in murky soil by the house,
and screw in a bulb to show
pages of Ondaatje's story
between Anna and Coop
after still no fucking sleep
or steady breathing, aching, soon
a ruckus of wings that disappear
with the pigeons in the morning.

III

A MOMENT

Early in the morning we shuffle

beyond lavender leaves fallen

from jacaranda trees laden with blooms

....

and a woman walks beneath them

her knee giving to one side as she moves

beneath such beauty

....

televisions along the road blaring

like monsters and you keep time to the tune

of *My Girl* or *Hurdy Gurdy Man* or *Concerto in G*,

....

these miracle moments

elegantly struck by love.

THE NEW MUSIC

In Disney Hall I sit by a man who loosens his tie

and kicks the side of my calf as he crosses his leg, a double
excuse me. The celebrity conductor strides to the center

of the stage, swings from audience veneration to his famous

musicians suited up in black clothes, erect spines, his breath
unheard as the white baton is raised. I sit above

the rhythm men with sticks striking bells, crystal glasses,
gongs trembling. Piano keys are played in a blur, struck

by a woman who glows with the precision of her maestro.

My mind flees its demons of circumstance, unconcerned
if the maker of the composition *meant it this way*

or if Philip Glass truly knows *those streams traveling
beneath the sound.* I leave my body, pinned to my seat by oboes,

French horns, string pings until there is the afterlife of dying
notes and one long fade quiets into the shuffle of the audience,

his and my thighs uncrossing, players sit poised
in atonal sheen, instruments down and our altered selves

surge with applause, applause until we rise up gleaming.

WHAT IF THE ANIMAL-SELF
BUCKS ME OUT OF THE CORRAL

what if
the violin bow grows a jagged edge and saws
the ballads of love into pieces, arias sliced from a jaw hinge

and what if we sigh into
the universal microphone and reverb
is bruised on its boomerang return and what if I relinquish

to the humans with blood
on my hands, learn to yield myself,
to be chameleon, undo the fixer, and what if need or want

gnaw holes in my dress until
they make my back bare, and I make a sly reach, then let go of my grip
        on slippery

land at the tree until free
to ride a quiet boat on the river and what
if new words beseech the body to change direction

to what was love
and what used to hold me rapt
under a blue moon, this is no longer what I mean, and what if

my path begins to teach skills of the grift
and all is mercurial, and what I know is damaged like a curdling,

and what if I drink tea
instead of sucking the mimic of poison

and what if I am surprised
by unfamiliar vision, and what if I go there?

HOW A NEW CENTURY SETTLES

Sea life is too warm, deserts overrun
by housing tracts thirty miles long

and the world looks on, indecision in its teeth,
the gnawed-up earth accepted like permanent fever.

How do we bite into a future without a return to the land?
Six million trees collapse.
30,000 species disappear a year,
their throats in our hands.

We disremember how we lived without
ovens, saunas, drugs for personality revisions,
shiny coins and condoms,
forgetting the sadness of forgetting.

There is a fan of furniture in the basement, a
collapse of groundcover—an elk falling off a mountain.

My face changes shape with age
and despair, but then there are days I look away
and the air lets loose to swipe clean what kills us.

A FIND

So, I want to take this walk, see—where earth is *au naturelle*
and traces of people are hidden, like lost quarters, a torn
                              corner of a scarf.

I tell my long-time guy who walks with me how we could
just keep going beyond town where mud-muck and trees

inspire wanderlust, a meeting of eagles and sky.
We stroll with a hip bump and a swerve, cruising past a café
                              lost to the days we met,

our plates untouched. People in shorts and skimpy
shirts in this heat scurry by and I ask if he hears the city's pain

as it mourns the empty stores, eyes shaded by our hands
                              to peer at what we have lost.

We trek to a darkening edge of the woods, our feet in mulch
unfamiliar to what we know, a secret garden, a beetle holding

its slick wings against its body all lit up, iridescent
                    in the glare of satellites, sun flares, a galaxy.

LOSING ROE

I imagine he might lift his head in a wave against the evening light, a gesture I never saw him do since I never saw him in the flesh and bone after he had barely begun to grow in me, undeveloped, unstirred, until he was a full human with a future head like a huge golden sky.

He will never know I let him go when I was too much like my mother who had just left the earth, and me lacking sense and a third eye to comprehend what a parent needs to give. I was deadly afraid how a son might perish, as if I could drop him from my hands or fail to find food, a place to bring him up alert or good or bad or saved.

I speak to him and say he would be a man of middle age now, maybe pissed at me or bringing flowers the way notes might have arrived in his hand from school, to say, *yes, he's a good boy, just a small slight incident to discuss*—and yet, only I would know he was living inside himself with mute grief.

I take a walk among the trees, perhaps a nod to how my son would have grown like a reed reaching out of a pond, and I walk farther into the city with throngs in the streets shouting for control of their own bodies. I walk with these women, one step, and another, pitching our voices to say straight up that sometimes a woman is unable to do everything when she knows she can't.

NOT INCLUDING THE ANIMALS

A boy picks up a gun his father
gave him and the father takes his son to a field

where they shoot bullets ten in a row into peach cans
        lined up and pelted
        until nothing is left but holes.

By the time the kid grows enough to make the gun
his own he likes the feel and praises the holy

miracle of distance and speed to kill things
        in case there is a need to eliminate threat

to his family. They grow large so he needs another gun
to keep his wife and children and dogs alive

        so maybe a gun for each person he has to save
        is the best advice. When there is a sound,

perhaps an animal raiding the yard, the man fires, but "only
a coyote" so he tosses the gun. Or better to bury it

in a spot he will remember under the dirt
disfigured by 400 million guns for 300 million people.

AND HERE WE GO AGAIN

A man follows the Mexican home
         along Apple Valley Highway

to his house where the chaser enters
                 and beats the Mexican,

screaming *I-ranian* as he leads him
into fresh blood on the Mexican's own floor

and there is pain of age with no regard
                         for wisdom,

         our sisters disappearing in Juarez,

apparition of a bullet in the neck, oblong
                 pills shaped like tiny

stadiums into our wide open
throats and I remember if a woman

                 who drags a goat
                 is slaughtered it is

a kind of genocide,
every war filling us longer than sorrow.

GORDON PARKS

Artists see with their hands and the nerves beneath
our skin, straight lines then swerve, as the eyes
kick away dirt to unbury a river flow of human
living. The photographer is a better portrait
than the subjects he shoots. No, not guns, not blades.
He smokes a pipe, his face beneath a cowboy hat
curled and shaped like a thought. He looks off
through fog behind his jean jacket, a lens that fractures
light droops from his neck, hands in his pockets
petting a soothing stone, white collar against black skin,
eyes taking in all that we have unearthed. We come alive
with clicks from a button-sized spot on the top of a black
case and its lens protruding to discover flit of eyes
and where the vision goes to find and pause gestures,
glances where true surprise and discovery light up,
to see ourselves in moods, his neck 112 years old today
bent a bit to close himself around the view. A mother
and child stand outside a theater with bowed heads.
At a dinner table, Martin Luther King, Stokely slumped
over images of Malcolm X, a boy and father in a field,
Rosa Parks defiant in no bullshit determined defiance.

SITTING AT MY DESK AS IF
I HAVE A JOB TO DO

It is not as it was. And he says,
of course not, and I tell him,
now we are a hunk of bones
shoving out rigorous pain like the aftermath

of a brawl. When I saw he could
dish out damage with a right hook—it wasn't
always like this—my hair sprouted
white strands like limp string. *What the…*

he would say from his lips dripping
judgment. I gather bread and avocado, and
the mailman needs an ear to speak
of his daughters, bilingual, but teens now,

and what should he do for them. His fingers fold
over a pile of solicitation that I flip into the recycle
can like cards into a bowl.

It is not as it was, as my soulmate
promises a gift and dinner, more
red-headed birds winging it past the window.

CORNERS OF A BOISTEROUS SKY

The bird rescuer says *birds like noise*. Suzanne Vega sang, *blood makes noise*, and wherever the beak or body takes us in our preening and turmoil there are untethered leaves and a crackle of branches as the winged ones touch down and circulations of blood scramble to feed the heart.

I never remember if people in a dream make noise—gulls flap above lovers shifting in sand— then I'm flying into a small town suddenly not my own—I mistrust an unfamiliar couple waving wildly—then I'm stepping inside as I get quickened from sleep.

The bird lady is named Karen and she opens rooms in her Victorian house, its walls of pigeons, finches and doves in cages stationed like furniture all the way up to the eaves. I lean close to the bars where birds fold their heads under damaged wings, and when injuries heal she tosses each bird back into the sky.

The night takes away the sun, hangs itself over the chatter of traffic, sky-high eucalyptus trees sighing like slow fans, and I dream I am deaf.

A PARK BENCH ON THE EDGE
OF THE UNIVERSITY

Sometimes a great idea might come rolling
to his feet like a ball, a widget broken from a wire.

He might look down from the bench. He might peer
forward as if the idea were a jewel or a sign and log it

away for a line with just the right detail for his pen
put to paper, enlightening the previously mundane.

Always autumn when we sat listening to birds
and sometimes a student drifted by, his head lowered

to his chest and the boy would nod the way men do,
and he'd nod back like a secret handshake or maybe

he'd send a question to me like *who is that, your
student or mine,* and I'd say *it's Ray.* He'd say how

the kid would walk through a symmetry of roses
to write of beauty and would brave the thorns

to get to the petals. His eyes radiated the palest blue
and women snuck glances, me facing some chick's

good-smelling hair tangled with mine as she'd close in
to ask, *You. Know him?* And sometimes *Yes,* or

silence to help them imagine. In 1907 hallways, kids
looked at him like seeing stars, his collar up in muted

sweater and always a shave, his students edge-of-
their-seats waiting for him to lope into the room and speak—

Hello, let's read some poems. The days I'd drive us
home first to his desk to drop the day's papers laid open

like a woman unfolded, I'd hand him tea, the quiet
jazz of Bill Evans, especially, Bill. Daffodils splayed

across the antique table. Always flowers as he'd push
off his loafers and lean back to sink into a wing-backed

chair, evening coming in like a fog. It was time—I understood
time when he didn't and I'd descend to the street, leave him

to feel the warmth of Darjeeling tea, to settle into himself,
into his mysterious, mischievous, most days, harmonious life.

Ralph Angel
1951—2020

MY BEAUTIFUL CAR

Sound fills the gulley and the gulley
is wet, small animals bend their heads
to the wreck. I cannot hear traffic
as the city dies from its errors, and the day
lies quiet like a hand inside a shirt. The air
is muggy, stiff as a bed, good enough to lie on,
to breathe in silence. Nothing looks the same—
rattled with wonder-wander of my mind as I veer
off from what is familiar—the man who
could do me in lounges by the broken stolen car.
I hear the steam, a continual crack of metal
and glass drips from my beautiful car, my gentle
and criminal man seeming to sleep. I hear him
exhale grunts I wouldn't make, too harsh
and gurgled, my stunned relief he isn't dead. My
red stinging hands reach for strange mercy. We are
alive again, no bones in unusual angles, minimal
blood, so I lift my head. His voice has taken in
gravel when I see him move. *Don't fuss over me,*
I know how to do this. There is sizzle up my spine when
he says, *there is possibility of fire, a splash of oil*
into leaps of flame. He moves, calls to me.
We are alive. Before noon I recall the words
let's drive up into the canyon. The grass is still
green, our bodies useless, but I do get up, brush off
the grime. We roll onto one side then push to crawl.
I'm not sure I can follow him as a big shift can harm
love. The hillside still trembles, and birds call out
in harmony with sirens, stink of defeat and gasoline.

EXCUSE ME WHILE I KISS THIS GUY
(A MONDEGREEN)

I push a scaly skin boot down on the accelerator when the radio says especially loud that Waylon is dead. In a shaky key from girlhood choirs, I sing about good-hearted women and still shiver like I'm out with no socks on, lapping the winter air like a bloodhound puppy over that almighty JQ, my Wyoming lover tall as Jon Voight with Stetson hat to match. Except *my* cowboy was a drug-dealing, whore-running gent with muscles on him worth a thousand grabs, nights with him miles from sleep and peace. But that New Year's Eve, I knew exactly where I was—front row table, Million Dollar Cowboy Bar with Waylon on the marquee, rubbing up to cowboy gangsters who exhale flattery and breathe in Cutty Sark. JQ, my Adonis with top hat of golden hair, wore a roll of green & white *in god we trust* with its shocker of zeroes next to the second gun he carried just in case. When the singing stopped & the crowd wound down from clapping & whistling & yelling his name we sashayed outside under the stars, where only the condemned move around a town like Jackson, steely air so still you could balance on it. Our posse roamed the ski-jock streets as one by one we went down harder than two-legged chairs, icy and knotty-pine sidewalks yanked from under us quick as fire from a Colt. The freeze traveled in like silver chips making us shimmy with lips running hit-n-miss at one another's mouths and Waylon howling with laughter that struck at the moon along the ridge of the Tetons. And so it went all night, falling down & crazy-speak, hours whirling from black to morning pinks that licked our sinfulness clean, all of us lucky to be sniffing out of the king crooner's hand. And even when that sonofabitch JQ dumped me in late spring I'd be consoled by Waylon singing velvety and deep as I leaned back, certain about those men who know how mold grows inside our character, how residue of civilization tends to uncork the worst in us, how, when those satin-throated boys say, *hey, honey, c'mon and dance with me,* I swear they mean it—they goddamn well really mean it.

REGRET IS LIKE SAWING WOOD WITH A SPOON

sometimes after midnight
I am tired
of it all.
—Sonia Sanchez

In the middle of the night when drugs and counting backward don't work, I come up with new experiments to drive insomnia back into its cave. The new thing that came to me one chilly night during "June gloom" when the rest of the country was slush in summer heat and rolling in the grass—perhaps smoking a little—was to blurt out words in a stream, starting with "A" and moving through the alphabet, avoiding sentence-sense that makes order of this life. When I feel my midsection ticking like an explosive in a briefcase I start my list with *acrobat*, then easily mumble through *beleaguered, cauliflower, danger, endemic,* and I know I could read a book from my stack, but other people's exploits gather like misdemeanors, urging me to sidle up to regret as if it is a living-breathing body, and no doubt *flammable*. Maybe I should live in a *geodesic* dome, remain a *hellion* as I sit up to slap a mosquito, blood ticking onto the sheet, and for days it will *irritate* me. Deep breaths and mantras, then nothing but *jags* of longing for the *keyboardist* who *lounged* around after we had sex from one century to the next on New Year's Eve 1999-2000, but the *misery* of recall is lousy in bed and now I can't drift off without knees behind knees, an arm across a torso. By 2am, I hate to be a *naysayer*, an *outcast*, this night *porous* like *quiescent* water slipping from skin, when there is the miracle of a drift into a doze and a hasty pace into *relinquish, stun-gun, talisman,* as I listen to the cars race along the boulevard with a leap into animal-counting but worry about them crossing the road. My mind *undulates* between *victory* and regret about not driving into good clean living, *x-asperated* I didn't dig in my heels or steer the wheel into the skid rather than *yaw* and *zigzag* into the guardrail. Mind churns, guilt, retraction, eyes open, *activate, biosphere, conscience…*

WE WERE JUST LIKE THAT

My mother handled the heaviest pain
with a hush in her throat

as she settled me in the garden
                short of breath, clearing out weeds.

                A crush of woe could land on her
like steel, like soulless tv when the days

ended and I would lie down and suck deeper into her.

Weather arrives with its stealth
blazing in change when I am chill under thin skin
and growing old without her. I misunderstand

how I am too much like her, how
                even meager
                        dampness reshapes soil.

Crosswise on my bed I look past the north side
of basic house construction, a glaze of windows

looking beyond that, a childhood in our courtyard
steeped in snow. Trees grew thirty feet high
                        after my mother was
                gone, murder

by her own hand, the body incinerated and abandoned

         beneath the life she died in. We were wild
together with furtive gestures, her face

              pure diamonds, our hands shiny
with new growth, and lately ghost sounds waft like weeds,
the dark air grazed in a bite and exhale of her, or its own, breath.

MOTHERS AND DAUGHTER

I carry pots of tulips and put them where
she asks and settle them beneath the sun. My mothers
come in a fit of calamity from corners in the dark,

the tall one leaning on a flowering pear, the dead one
murmuring regret, wayward voices
speaking of what chance feels like slapped

against the cool air. My father wooed
the mothers, once when everyone was young, and D.
when he was older, eternally handsome
until the year he forgot the words, his

thinker's engine failing. Anger rises
and I see the mother who ages with me
pick up her watering hose, sniffing the sage
as it fills a door into the house. My muscles move

me to where the final mother's cats are buried.
I watch how she plants her bulbs, digging deeper,
the mother who gave me life and magic to live through

ramshackle days sinks into soil like the rods
that deter lightning. D. lugs a clay pot like dragging
children from danger, the mother in memory faint

beneath a Japanese maple where light comes
as the dying leaves fall away, flowers loose
on their stems, weary, always draped across my arms.

BERNADETTE, TO THE TUNE OF *BERNADETTE*

She was a legend when we met, my friend charming
my hand to take Bernadette's hand outstretched
from her body that leaned and swayed at six
feet tall as she bent a bit to greet me and we sang

our names under a vengeance of the sun. Tonight
she claims she is ready, and asks for ice chips
rather than morphine, her head fortified but her

neck gives way, her beautiful face curved to her chest
as though she can scheme her way out of this. Yeah,
but let me tell you how she drowns flowers in water

under the faucet that feeds them. At the end of
the cul-de-sac is a crossroad with an Elfin Forest
boardwalk slicing a slinky voyage into pygmy oaks,

sagebrush, manzanita, spiky foxtails, gooseberry,
everything she touched, dogs yanking leashes,
aromas making them shimmy in nettle and cattails

before meandering home with a sheen on the bay,
sunset diffusing her silhouette into mist. Our feet
ground dirt into kitchen tile as we clicked stems
from spinach leaves, and I could see how she would

always be in love with him as she brushed his arm
gliding past bread board to lettuce spinner, his hand
shaking a pan of oil on the stove. Her deep brown
hair tumbled then, quiet water down her back—

unlike the tight cap it's been shaved to, thinner
than crepe paper. The room crowds
with people from childhood, cousins from France,

our hips settled, ready to sit with her.
and everyone repeating greetings with Bernadette
holding her hands. He kisses her with a devotional
wink and she smiles past strain feeling best-laid plans
change the way balm becomes gunfire. She asks
if he might rearrange the room so everyone will

have chairs around the bed as if arranged to tell her
stories, and we do. The air moves her chest,
her limbs narrow as rope, vision keen and turned

to the love he shows. She would love to show
her love, too, if only she could reclaim her
body, fold at the waist and fondle tulips newly
opened like a window, move her hands through his hair.

DAYS OF WAR

Across a turbulent sea
the population becomes refugees.

Sandstorms landlock
borders strained at their seams, fences
breached, bombardment fled.

I drive away
from the country fields
through a sunset simmering in softest
orange as if fire is a gentle invention.

Landscapes stutter past tract homes
behind automatic gates.
Somewhere a boy blows a tire on his bike

and is saved by a gardener snipping
roses with an explosion of blooms. Constant,

in peripheral vision are global invasions,
starvation in Yemen, Gaza,

Iraq, Syria, Sudan, Ukraine, the children

of the world toting bags that carry their food
and somewhere a rolled blanket to make a bed,
to spread trinkets laid out for coin.

I drive into the mouth of my insecurity,
garage beside dogs in a tussle on the lawn,
then growls calm, the quiet like unmarred snow.

Like this, like this.

ACKNOWLEDGMENTS

We are grateful to the following people whose generosity made the posthumous publication of this book possible. Profound thanks to Sigrid Burton and Tod Burton, who donated funding for this book. Thank you to Susie Parry and Sandra Adair for finding the password to Jan's computer as well as the last hard copy drafts. Thanks to Holaday Mason for midwifing the book into publication, to James Cushing for collating and proofing, Sarah Maclay for proofing the forward, and David St. John for his loving tribute. A resounding thank you to the poet and publisher Gail Wronsky for astutely editing and ordering the final manuscript. What Books Press, you are champions for the longevity of innovative writing and thought. Thank you to Gronk for the artwork that appears on the cover, and to ash good for the stunning book design. And last, but never last—thank you Jan Wesley for writing and rewriting these poems right until the end.

—*The Venice Collective*

WHAT BOOKS PRESS

AN IMPRINT OF

THE GLASS TABLE

COLLECTIVE

LOS ANGELES

WHAT BOOKS feature cover art by Los Angeles painter, printmaker, muralist, and theater and performance artist GRONK. A founding member of ASCO, Gronk collaborates with the LA and Santa Fe Operas and the Kronos Quartet. His work is found in the Corcoran, Smithsonian, LACMA, and Riverside Art Museum's Cheech Marin collection.

As a small, independent press, we urge our readers to support independent publishers and booksellers. This is easily done by visiting our website, WhatBooksPress.com, where you can purchase books directly from us or from Bookshop.org

Figures of Wood
MARÍA PÉREZ-TALAVERA
TRANSLATED BY PAUL FILEV
NOVEL

A Plea for Secular Gods: Elegies
BRYAN D. PRICE
POEMS

Nightfall Marginalia
SARAH MACLAY
POEMS

Romance World
TAMAR PERLA CANTWELL
STORIES

2022

No One Dies in Palmyra Ohio
HENRY ELIZABETH CHRISTOPHER
NOVEL

Us Clumsy Gods
ASH GOOD
POEMS

Skeletal Lights From Afar
FORREST ROTH
FLASH FICTION/PROSE POEMS

That Blue Trickster Time
AMY UYEMATSU
POEMS

2021

Pyre
MAUREEN ALSOP
POEMS

What Falls Away Is Always
KATHARINE HAAKE &
GAIL WRONSKY, EDITORS
ESSAYS

*The Eight Mile
Suspended Carnival*
REBECCA KUDER
NOVEL

Game
M.L. WILLIAMS
POEMS

2020

No, Don't
ELENA KARINA BYRNE
POEMS

One Strange Country
STELLA HAYES
POEMS

*Remembering Dismembrance:
A Critical Compendium*
DANIEL TAKESHI KRAJSE
NOVEL

Keeping Tahoe Blue
ANDREW TONKAVICH
STORIES

2019

Time Crunch
CATHY COLMAN
POEMS

Whole Night Through
L.I. HENLEY
POEMS

Echo Under Story
KATHERINE SILVER
NOVEL

Decoding Sparrows
MARIANO ZARO
POEMS

2018

Interrupted by the Sea
PAUL LIEBER
POEMS

The Headwaters of Nirvana
BILL MOHR
POEMS

2012

The Mermaid at the Americana Arms Motel
A.W. DEANNUNTIS
NOVEL

The Time of Quarantine
KATHARINE HAAKE
NOVEL

Frottage & Even As We Speak
MONA HOUGHTON
NOVELLAS

West of Eden:
A Life in 21ˢᵗ Century Los Angeles
CHUCK ROSENTHAL
MAGIC JOURNALISM

2010

Master Siger's Dream
A.W. DEANNUNTIS
NOVEL

Other Countries
RAMÓN GARCÍA
POEMS

A Giant Claw
GRONK
ESSAY BY GAIL WRONSKY
SPANISH TRANSLATION
BY ALICIA PARTNOY
ART

Coyote O'Donohughe's
History of Texas
CHUCK ROSENTHAL
NOVEL

So Quick Bright Things
GAIL WRONSKY
BILINGUAL, SPANISH TRANSLATION
BY ALICIA PARTNOY
POEMS

2009

Bling & Fringe
(The L.A. Poems)
MOLLY BENDALL &
GAIL WRONSKY
POEMS

April, May, and So On
FRANÇOIS CAMOIN
STORIES

One of Those Russian Novels
KEVIN CANTWELL
POEMS

The Origin of Stars
& Other Stories
KATHARINE HAAKE
STORIES

Lizard Dream
KAREN KEVORKIAN
POEMS

Are We Not There Yet?
Travels in Nepal,
North India, and Bhutan
CHUCK ROSENTHAL
MAGIC JOURNALISM

WHAT
BOOKS
PRESS

LOS ANGELES

www.ingramcontent.com/pod-product-compliance
Lightning Source LLC
Chambersburg PA
CBHW031254120626
46545CB00007B/2812